Creative HANDPAINTED BEARS 2

by Annette Stevenson

A J.B. Fairfax Press Publication

CONTENTS

ACKNOWLEDGMENTS

A huge thankyou to my husband, Peter, for your never-ending love and support; and to my children – Jessica, Caitlyn, Samuel and Georgina – whom I love and cherish.

A very special thankyou to David and Norma, for the wonderful wood pieces in this book and the special friendship that we share.

To my students Gwen, Kay, Fay, Karen, Maria, Donna, Kerry, Mary, Ordette, Gillian, Barbara, Val, DeDe, Lynne and Rhonda, thankyou for the many hours of fun and laughter that we share.

A special thankyou to June and Mary from Romantique, Cheryl from Wood Be Crafty and Sue from VADA.

Thankyou to Judy Poulos and Morgan D'Arcy from J.B. Fairfax Press, without whose help and support this book would never have happened.

Thankyou to my special friends Diane, Sally, Pauline, Val and John for the long chats on the phone.

EDITORIAL
Managing Editor: Judy Poulos
Editorial Assistant: Ella Martin
Production Editor: Heather Straton
Photography: Neil Lorimer
Styling: Judy Ostergard
Illustrations: Lesley Griffith

DESIGN AND PRODUCTION
Production Manager: Anna Maguire
Production Coordinator: Meredith Johnston
Design: Jenny Nossal
Cover Design: Jenny Pace
Design Manager: Drew Buckmaster
Graphic Designer: Sheridan Packer

Published by J.B. Fairfax Press, an imprint of LibertyOne Media Group Pty Limited
80-82 McLachlan Ave
Rushcutters Bay NSW, Australia 2011
A.C.N. 078 084 447

JBFP 481
CREATIVE HANDPAINTED BEARS 2
ISBN 1 86343 370 8

Formatted by J.B. Fairfax Press
Film Separations by Four Colour Graphics
Printed by Toppan Printing Company, Hong Kong
© LibertyOne Media Group Pty Limited 1999
This book is copyright. No part may be reproduced by any process without the written permission of the publisher. Enquiries should be made in writing to the publisher.

DISTRIBUTION AND SALES
Australia: J.B. Fairfax Press
Ph: (02) 9361 6366 Fax: (02) 9360 6262
Web: http://www.jbfp.com.au
USA: Quilters' Resource Inc
2211 North Elston Ave
Chicago, Ill 60614
Ph: (773) 278 5695 Fax: (773) 278 1348

STOCKISTS
All the wood pieces in this book are available from:

Romantique
68 Milton Parade
Malvern, Victoria 3144
Ph: (03) 9822 5293

VADA
1132 Toorak Road
Camberwell, Victoria 3124
Ph: (03) 9809 2788

Wood Be Crafty
58 Aberdeen Road
Macleod, Victoria 3085
Ph: (03) 9458 2582

DEDICATION

This book is dedicated to my mum, Kate McNally, who has always given me the love, support and encouragement to allow me to achieve my life's goals. Thanks Mum.

ABOUT THE AUTHOR

Annette Stevenson is a Victorian-based decorative artist, who teaches weekly classes at Romantique in Malvern. She has a wide and varied painting style but her passion is painting teddies and roses, and this is what her many students enjoy the most. She has worked in art-and-craft-related fields since leaving college with an arts degree. Her ever-changing painting styles and techniques have kept her students returning to class year after year.

Annette travels extensively around Victoria and interstate, conducting workshops on how to paint her cute and cuddly bears, their intricate clothes and floral adornments.

Her first book *Handpainted Bears* was written to introduce you to the wonderful world of bear painting, and is an ideal companion for *Handpainted Bears 2*. She has designed and painted découpage papers and is currently working on a range of gift cards and a calendar.

INTRODUCTION

This book is for everyone who loves teddy bears – to paint, draw or just to look at. I have written this book with the view of inspiring you to create your own collection of furry friends to treasure and enjoy with your own family.

Many things inspire my painting, but it is my large bear family that offers me the greatest inspiration of all. Wherever I am in my home there is always a furry friend to talk to or to cuddle; they all hold very special memories in my heart and family.

In my first book, I briefly touched on some of the ways that I have developed to paint bear fur, this book expands greatly on these styles and many new bear styles have grown from the previous ones. They are all painted with a loving attention to detail and each has its own unique personality.

I cannot remember a time when I didn't want to draw and paint my family of bears – I hope that this book will inspire you to do the same. I wish you many hours of enjoyment and success with these projects, and I am sure that you will find immense satisfaction in your achievements.

Annette

MATERIALS

PAINTS

I use a variety of brands of paints for my projects as each has certain colours and qualities that I like. Jo Sonja's Artists Acrylic Gouache has a thick consistency that is wonderful for bear fur. DecoArt Americana has so many colours to choose from. This paint is slightly thinner than Jo Sonja's Gouache and is ideal for flowers and transparent lace. Matisse Professional Artists Acrylic Colour has beautiful rich colours for clothes and trims.

PALETTE

I use a dry, waxed palette as I prefer the paint to be slightly dry for painting these bears. Small puddles of paint are preferable to large ones so they don't dry up completely before I have to renew my palette.

BRUSHES

You will need a variety of flat brushes for base coating and painting. I usually buy Neef brushes as they perform well and last a long time. The sable flat brushes are excellent for floating, shading, highlighting and painting lace. I paint all the liner work using a size 1 short liner brush from Neef, series 992. These brushes retain their fine point for painting delicate lace and frills. For the furry bears, I use the Neef 440 deerfoot brushes in a variety of sizes, according to the size of the bear I am painting. For the long, shaggy-haired bears, I use Neef 975 rake brushes. The feathering filbert, number 989 is excellent for creating curly looped fur, straight or shaggy fur.

PAPER TOWEL

It is always a great idea to have a few pieces of paper towel beside you when you paint, to blot brushes on or to wipe off excess paint.

OTHER ITEMS

- white chalk (for drawing in roses or clothes)
- stylus (for transferring the designs or making dots)
- graphite paper in blue and white (for transferring designs)
- kneadable eraser
- artgum eraser
- sharpener
- black lead pencil
- cotton buds
- soft cloth (for antiquing and staining)
- fine sandpaper, 320 grade
- coarse sandpaper, 120 grade
- tack cloth

Other supplies used in this book are:
- gilding milk
- gold leaf
- soft, white gloves
- candle (any colour)
- textile medium
- Treasure Gold
- mop brush
- plastic kitchen wrap

PREPARATION AND FINISHING

BASE PAINTING

I use a good quality 1" base coating brush and sand lightly between coats. Depending on the colour you are using, apply two coats for a dark base coat and three or four coats for a light base coat.

ANTIQUING

I only antique those pieces I have base painted with a pale colour, as this gives a gentle aged effect that would normally take years to achieve.

To antique, first apply an even coat of antiquing patina, using a soft cloth, then rub Burnt Umber oil paint over the entire surface to be antiqued. With a clean cloth gently wipe this off, making sure that the edges are soft. It is nice to have the corners or along an outside edge slightly darker.

STAINING

I like to stain the wood, such as pine, so that the beautiful grain shows through. I use Liquitex Acrylic Wood Stain in a variety of colours. Dark Walnut and Cherry mixed together will create a lovely dark stain; adding more or less of one colour will bring more red or walnut into the stain. Because the Liquitex stains are like gel and they penetrate the pine quickly, I like to seal pine pieces first with a sealer base. For this, mix equal parts of Jo Sonja's Retarder, Jo Sonja's All Purpose Sealer and Brown Earth acrylic paint. Brush this mixture onto the surface, then wipe it off with a rag in the direction of the wood grain.

GILDING

Gilding is a lovely finish for picture frames or the edges of boxes. Begin by base painting the area to be gilded with two coats of acrylic paint in a colour to match the project. Sand this really well, then apply a thin, even coat of gilding milk. Allow this to dry until the surface is just tacky – this usually takes about five to ten minutes.

Apply the gold leaf in small overlapping pieces to cover the area to be gilded. Always wear a pair of soft gloves when handling the gold leaf, so that your hands do not become too sticky and covered with gold leaf. Using a soft-bristled brush, rub gently over the gold leaf to remove any loose pieces. It is a lovely effect to see the base paint showing through the cracks in the gold leaf. Finally, you can antique the gilded frame lightly to tone down the gold colour.

VARNISHING

On most of my pieces, I use Cabots Crystal Clear Varnish in a satin finish. Apply three or four coats of this product, sanding lightly between coats. I always keep one brush just for varnishing and I never wash this brush. I keep it suspended in a large jar of water and rinse it out each time I use it. If the piece has been antiqued, I use J.W.'s Right Step Satin Varnish as this is the only water-based varnish that will adhere to an oil-based finish.

SMUDGED BACKGROUNDS

With these backgrounds you can really have fun and play with your colours. I usually start with a couple of coats of a pale beige, then sand this well. Next, I apply a watery coat of the same colour and crosshatch a couple of other colours onto the paint while the background is still wet. Finally, I soften where the different colours meet, using a mop brush. It is important to really smudge the colours together. Using a touch of the same colours in the painted design will tie the whole picture together.

BRUSH TECHNIQUES

I always float the shading and highlighting using a flat brush that fits comfortably into the design area. A 1/2" flat brush has also been used to paint most of the bears' clothes.

Dip the brush into the water container and gently blot it on the paper towel to remove the excess water. Dip the corner of the brush into the puddle of paint and blend this well on your palette to soften. When floating shading or highlighting always use the brush flat with the paint side of the brush closest to where you need to shade or highlight. Where two shade or highlight colours are called for, pick up a touch of each colour on the same side of the brush and mix them together on the palette. It is better to do this than to mix up a puddle of the colour, as the variation in colour every time you load your brush will add extra light and dark values to the finished painting.

TRANSFERRING THE DESIGN

The designs are either with the project or on the Pull Out Pattern Sheet. Some need to be enlarged on a photocopier and are marked accordingly. Once the design is the correct size, trace it onto tracing paper. Position the pattern, then slide a sheet of suitably coloured graphite paper in between the tracing and the surface to be painted. Trace over the design, using a stylus, to transfer the design to the piece.

FURRY BEAR

This bear is a furry little fellow with a long snout. He can be painted with a round muzzle or as in the workboard opposite with the highlight above the nose flowing into the head.

He can be painted in many colour combinations. In my teaching travels I have seen some very interesting combinations, such as blue, burgundy and pale green.

He is painted using three deerfoot brushes, one for the base colour, one for the shade and one for the highlights. I paint this bear in sections – for example, the head or the tummy or the arms – so that the paint stays wet while I soften and play with the colours.

PALETTE

Jo Sonja's Artists Acrylic Gouache: Raw Sienna, Fawn, Brown Earth, Yellow Oxide, Warm White, Burnt Umber, Smoked Pearl, Burnt Sienna.

PAINTING

STEP ONE

Note: Depending on my background colour, I don't usually pre-base paint my bears – I stipple the fur straight on to the bear. If the background is really dark, I apply a quick background of the base colour using a flat brush.

Using the three deerfoot brushes and working on one section at a time, apply the fur. Stipple or pounce lightly over the bear using Raw Sienna and a touch of Fawn with the first brush. Mix this colour on the brush, as this will give the bear a slight colour variation.

STEP TWO

Stipple the shadows, using the second brush with Brown Earth. These shadows need to be darkest inside the ears, along the edges of the snout, under the chin, to place the tummy in front or behind the arms (depending how your bear is sitting) and on the pads of the feet. It is important to soften these shadows as you paint each section, so that there is no definite line of colour.

STEP THREE

Finally, add the highlights using the third deerfoot brush. The highlights are Yellow Oxide, a touch of Fawn and of Warm White. Very lightly pounce the brush along the edges of the bear. It is important to see all the colours used in the finished bear. The bear can be left at this stage or a final wisp of fur can be added, as described in Step four.

STEP FOUR

Using the highlight mix and a touch more Warm White, mix with water to a thin consistency, paint short wispy strokes with a liner brush over the stippled fur – these are strongest on the highlighted edges of the bear with just a few strokes in towards the shadowed areas.

STEP FIVE

Paint the eyes and the nose in Burnt Umber, using the liner brush. The eyes are round and are placed where the shadows on the snout end. Highlight the eyes with a soft float of Warm White on the left-hand side and a touch on the upper right-hand side, and on the nose.

VARIATIONS

Other variations for this bear are:
1 For a light bear, base paint with Yellow Oxide, shade with Burnt Sienna and highlight with Yellow Oxide and Warm White.
2 For a cream-coloured bear, base paint with Fawn, shade with Fawn and Brown Earth and highlight with Fawn and Smoked Pearl.
3 For a mustard-coloured bear, base paint with Raw Sienna, shade with Brown Earth and highlight with Yellow Oxide and Warm White.
4 For a darker bear, base paint with Burnt Sienna, shade using a brush mix of Brown Earth and Burnt Umber, and highlight with Yellow Oxide or a brush mix of Yellow Oxide, Warm White and Burnt Sienna.

OLD, MUCH LOVED BEAR

This old fellow, Big Ted, is one of my favourites and he looks great painted with a group of bears that have lots of different fur styles, as on the hat box on page 70.

He can be painted with rips and tears, with his stuffing hanging out or an eye missing. We all remember a favourite bear from our childhood that looked just like Big Ted.

This type of old bear is painted with no fur at all – just the holes where the fur has worn away.

PALETTE

Jo Sonja's Artists Acrylic Gouache: Yellow Oxide, Gold Oxide, Brown Earth, Warm White, Burnt Sienna, Burnt Umber
Jo Sonja's Clear Glazing Medium

STEP ONE

Load a flat brush with Yellow Oxide and base coat the bear.

STEP TWO

Side-load the same brush with Gold Oxide and float in the shading. The shading serves to section the bear, separating the tummy from the arms, around the muzzle, inside the ears, under the chin, and to define the pads on the feet.

STEP THREE

Repeat Step two, using Brown Earth to add extra depth under the chin, on the foot pads and inside the ears.

STEP FOUR

Side-load the same brush with Warm White and float a few highlights onto the bear – on the top of the head, ears and muzzle, and on his big, fat tummy.

STEP FIVE

Mix a small amount of Burnt Sienna with clear glazing medium in a ratio of 1:3. Making sure that the areas are dry, and working on one area at a time, base paint over the previous work. Work very quickly so that the maximum effect can be obtained from this next step. Lay a kitchen wipe, calico or paper towel over the wet area and rub gently, then lift it off and see the small pattern that remains. If you are not happy with the effect, recoat with the glaze mixture and try again. Allow this to dry really well.

STEP SIX

Side-load a flat brush – one that you are comfortable working with – in Burnt Umber and redefine the shadows, making sure that there are a few lumps and bumps here and there to give Big Ted a pre-loved look. He could be left at this stage or you could add some liner work in Burnt Umber around the edges.

STEP SEVEN

Add some lines in Burnt Umber for his eyes and nose, a few stitching lines around any shaded patches and you have your own old, well-remembered Big Ted from years gone by.

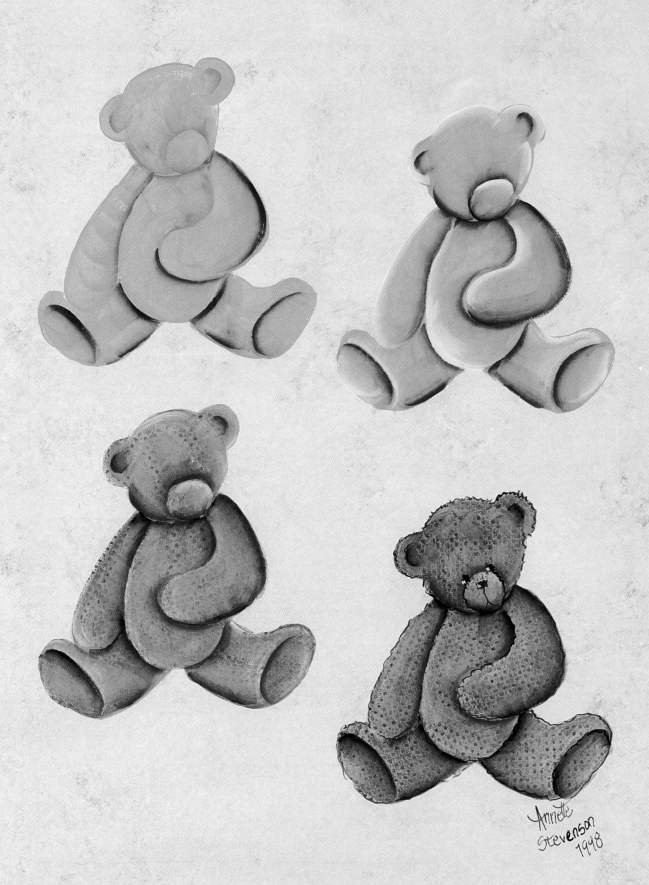

Annette
Stevenson
1998

SHAGGY, LONG-HAIRED BEAR

This type of bear fur can create many different bear styles. It takes a little more practice to achieve a pleasing look than with the furry bear style, but the result is worth the effort. A rake brush can be used to create straight fur or really curly fur.

You can change the colours of this bear when it is dry by glazing with Burnt Sienna for a darker bear or Yellow Oxide for a lighter bear. Try some colour variations of your own to see what effects you can achieve. Have fun and persevere, as she really is a gorgeous bear when finished.

The fur is painted using two rake brushes and lots of little lines to make her look soft and cuddly. I use clear glazing medium to help blend the paint and give me a longer time to 'play' with it.

The paint is loaded onto the tip of the brush only and used very lightly in a criss-cross manner to create the tiny wisps of fur.

Use the first brush for the first and second shade colours and the second brush for the first and second highlight colours.

Remember to complete each section of the bear before beginning another section.

PALETTE

Jo Sonja's Artists Acrylic Gouache:
  Raw Sienna, Gold Oxide, Brown
  Earth, Yellow Oxide, Warm White,
  Burnt Umber
Jo Sonja's Clear Glazing Medium

PAINTING

Note: The background colour determines whether a separate base coat is needed. If one is needed, block this in with a flat brush using Raw Sienna.

STEP ONE

Using Raw Sienna and a touch of the glazing medium, paint one section at a time – for example, the tummy or the head or the arms etc.

STEP TWO

Load the first rake brush with a small amount of the glazing medium and Gold Oxide. Apply the shading using short choppy strokes blending into the base colour, so that there is no definite line where the two colours meet.

STEP THREE

Wipe the brush on paper towel. Load the tip of the brush with the second shade colour, Brown Earth. The second shade colour is used to add extra depth in a few places, such as under the chin, inside the ears, and on the pads of the feet and where the legs join on to the body.

STEP FOUR

Using the second rake brush loaded with the glazing medium and Yellow Oxide, start to build up the highlights. These are painted from the outside of the bear working in towards the shaded areas. Use the brush in a flicking motion, creating lots of fine lines.

STEP FIVE

Wipe the brush, then pick up a small amount of Warm White. Continue to flick the brush softly to the very outside edges of the bear.

STEP SIX

The pads of the feet are base-painted with Raw Sienna. Side-load the same brush with a small amount of Brown Earth and float this around the edge of the pads.

STEP SEVEN

The eyes and nose are painted with a liner brush and Burnt Umber. Paint lots of small connecting lines so that you end up with an uneven shape, which makes it look like some of the fur is falling across the eyes.

Annette
Stevenson
1998

ROSES AND PANSIES

These roses are meant to be a suggestion of a rose rather than a complicated perfect representation of a rose. Relax, and play with the paint to create a soft, feathered rose.

ROSES

PALETTE

DecoArt Americana Acrylic Paint: Buttermilk, Dusty Rose, French Mocha

Jo Sonja's Artists Acrylic Gouache: Teal Green, Warm White

Matisse Professional Artists Acrylic Colour, Burgundy

STEP ONE

Double load a 1/2" flat brush with Buttermilk and Dusty Rose, then blend this well on the palette to create a third tone where the two colours meet. Base paint the bowl of the rose with the cream towards the top. The bowl is a C-stroke: slide down, glide across and slide up. Feather in the top petals, keeping them light and fluffy, and block in the side and bottom petals with the cream to the outside.

STEP TWO

Side-load the dirty brush with French Mocha and a touch of Burgundy. Float some extra depth into the throat of the rose, onto the lower edge of the bowl and on the side petals closest to the bowl.

For the white roses on Meg's hat on page 61, I add a touch of Pine Green shading here and there, at this stage.

STEP THREE

Highlight the rose with a dry-brushed method, using Buttermilk. Using a dry brush, load a tiny amount of paint onto the tip of the brush. These strokes are very light flicks of the brush, running in the direction of the petals. I usually add a couple to each of the side petals and a touch to the edge of the bottom petal. Reinforce the highlights with a touch of Warm White.

STEP FOUR

Paint the leaves with the same brush, loaded with a mix of Teal Green and Buttermilk. Put the brush down flat, twist up onto the chisel edge and lift off. Paint the stems and veins using the chisel edge of the brush and Teal Green.

STEP FIVE

Paint the buds using a mix of Teal Green and Buttermilk. Start with a small C-stroke, then make a larger C-stroke, then fill in the top edges. Float a touch of the deepest rose colour inside the top area of the bud.

PANSIES

PALETTE

Jo Sonja's Artists Acrylic Gouache: Paynes Gray, Teal Green, Warm White, Carbon Black, Yellow Oxide

Matisse Professional Artists Acrylic Colours: Burgundy, Antique Green

DecoArt Americana Acrylic Paint, Buttermilk

STEP ONE

Mix two or three values of Burgundy, Paynes Gray and Buttermilk – these colours make a beautiful muted purple when mixed.

STEP TWO

Load a 1/2" flat brush fully in the middle-value colour and side-load with a touch of Buttermilk. Blend these colours well on the palette and begin to stroke in the petals. Start with the two back ones, then the side ones and lastly, the large front petal. Pull the brush in the direction of the arrows on the step-by-step workboard. Each petal is painted in one stroke from the outside in.

STEP THREE

While the petals are still wet, pick up a touch more Buttermilk and highlight the edges of some of the petals. Also, add some of the dark-value purple to separate the petals.

STEP FOUR

I also add a soft float of Yellow Oxide to one side of the front petal. A dry-brushed highlight of Antique Green is also a nice variation to add to a couple of the flowers.

STEP FIVE

Add fine Carbon Black lines to the front and side petals, radiating out from the centre. Add a Yellow Oxide dot for the centre and two Warm White commas for the centre of the flower.

STEP SIX

Paint the leaves using a mix of Teal Green and Antique Green. Place the brush down, then pull it slightly outwards, twist and lift off to form a point. Paint the veins using Teal Green and a liner brush.

Annette
Stevenson
1998

BEARLY BEACH

This beach scene was inspired by my visit to teach at the Sea Which Craft shop
in Port Noarlunga. Helen, the owner, had so many beachside things
around her studio that they inspired me to paint this project.
I hope you have fun painting this bright beach scene.

MATERIALS

Craftwood book box, 23 cm x 28 cm
   x 5 cm (9 in x 11 in x 2 in)
Flat brushes: $1/2$", 1", $3/8$", $1/4$", $1/8$"
Short liner brush, size 1
Deerfoot brushes: $1/4$" (one), $1/8$" (two)
Stylus
Tracing paper
Graphite paper, white
Varnishing brush, 1"
Sandpaper, 320 grade
Tack cloth
Cabots Crystal Clear Satin Varnish
Jo Sonja's Artists Acrylic Gouache:
   Raw Sienna, Burnt Sienna, Brown
   Earth, Yellow Oxide, Turners
   Yellow, Warm White, Burnt Umber,
   Ultramarine, Paynes Gray, Aqua,
   Brilliant Green, Rich Gold
Matisse Professional Artists Acrylic
   Colour: Burgundy, Aqua Green
   Light, Powder Blue
DecoArt Americana Acrylic Paint:
   Teal Green, Country Red

PREPARATION

See the painting design on pages
22–23.

STEP ONE

Using the 1" flat brush, base paint the
inside of the box with a brush mix of
Ultramarine and Powder Blue. This
looks best if the two colours are a
little streaky.

STEP TWO

Paint the 'pages' inside the book with
two coats of Yellow Oxide.

STEP THREE

The front cover (inside and out) and
the back cover are painted as the sand
and the sky.

On your palette, have Yellow Oxide,
Raw Sienna, Turners Yellow, Warm
White, Powder Blue, Aqua Green Light
and Ultramarine. Have a container of
water and some paper towels handy.
Working on one area at a time, base
paint the sand with a thick coat of
Yellow Oxide. Gradually streak some
Raw Sienna, then Turners Yellow, then
a touch of Warm White across the sand
area. Note that the extra Raw Sienna
shading is painted after the bears have
been painted. Wash and dry the brush.

STEP FOUR

Repeat Step three, using the blue
colours on your palette to paint
the sky.

STEP FIVE

Sand all the painted areas lightly and
wipe with a tack cloth.

STEP SIX

Trace the design, then transfer it onto
the box, using the graphite paper.

PAINTING

CLOUDS

Using the $1/2$" flat brush, pick up a touch
of Warm White and fluff in the
clouds. These strokes need to be short
and choppy.

FRONT COVER

Note: For the painting of these cute
little beach bears, I have used the $1/4$"
deerfoot brush for basecoating and
one of the $1/8$" deerfoot brushes for
shading and highlighting.

STEP ONE

Bear relaxing on a deck chair: Paint
this little bear following the instructions
for the Furry Bear on page 8. Base
paint, using Raw Sienna, shade with
Brown Earth and highlight with a mix of
Yellow Oxide and Warm White.

STEP TWO

Deck chair: Paint the chair with two
coats of Warm White, using the $1/4$" flat
brush. Side-load the brush with a
touch of Burnt Umber and float on the
shadows. Add a couple of streaks to
simulate a wood grain. Side-load the
same brush with Warm White and add
extra strong highlights to the edges of
the chair.

STEP THREE

Umbrella: Base paint the umbrella sections with Warm White and Turners Yellow, alternating the two colours. Using Raw Sienna on the white sections and Burnt Sienna on the yellow sections, float in a little shading along the edges. Add a floated highlight to the lower edges of the yellow sections with a brush mix of Turners Yellow and Warm White.

Base paint the handle using Brown Earth, and paint the knob at the top with a mix of Burgundy and Country Red.

Paint the fine detail lines using Aqua on the white sections and Burgundy on the yellow sections.

STEP FOUR

T-shirt: Base paint the T-shirt with two coats of Turners Yellow. Shade with Raw Sienna, then highlight with Turners Yellow and Warm White. Paint the fine stripes with watery Warm White.

STEP FIVE

Shorts: Base paint with Aqua. Shade with a float of Aqua and Teal Green. Highlight the edges with a mix of Aqua and Warm White. This needs to be definite along the edge of the front leg to define the two legs of the shorts.

STEP SIX

Sunglasses: Base the frames with a mix of Burgundy and Country Red. Using the liner brush and watery Burnt Umber, paint in the glasses.

STEP SEVEN

Beach ball: Base paint the stripes on the ball using alternating stripes of Turners Yellow and Aqua. Float just a touch of Teal Green onto the top of each Aqua stripe. Paint a fine Warm White line between each stripe and a Burgundy line in the centre of the Aqua ones. Paint the flowers with dots, using the stylus – Aqua for the petals and Burgundy for the centres.

STEP EIGHT

Bear sunbaking on a towel: Paint this little bear following the Furry Bear instructions on page 8. Base paint with a mix of Burnt Sienna and Raw Sienna, then shade with Brown Earth and Burnt Sienna. Highlight with Burnt Sienna, Yellow Oxide and Warm White.

STEP NINE

Towel: Paint the towel with Aqua Green Light. Float the shading using a touch of the base colour and Teal Green. Float a highlight along the edge with the base colour and Warm White. Paint the fringe with Warm White, using the liner brush.

STEP TEN

Bathers: Paint the bathers with a mix of Powder Blue and Ultramarine. Float in the shading, using Paynes Gray, paying particular attention to the front leg. Highlight with a soft float of Powder Blue. Paint the stripes with watery Turners Yellow.

STEP ELEVEN

Bucket and spade: Paint with a mix of Powder Blue and Ultramarine. Float the shading with Paynes Gray, then highlight with a float of Powder Blue. Using the ³/₈" flat brush loaded with Turners Yellow and Warm White, fluff in the sand spilling out of the bucket.

STEP TWELVE

Beach house on the left: Base paint the first beach house with Turners Yellow and shade with Burnt Sienna. Paint the door with Aqua Green Light and shade around the edges with Teal Green. Paint the roof and frame around the door with Paynes Gray. Paint the lifebuoy with Warm White and Country Red.

STEP THIRTEEN

Beach house in the middle: Base paint in Powder Blue. Paint the stripes with Turners Yellow, using the ¹/₄" flat brush moistened with water. Float under each yellow stripe with Ultramarine. Paint the door with Country Red, and the roof, flag and door frame with Warm White. Paint the flagpole with Brown Earth and the stripe on the flag with Brilliant Green.

Note the wood grain on the legs of the deck chair

STEP FOURTEEN

Beach house on the right: Paint the roof with Country Red with Burgundy shading. Paint the house with Warm White with Country Red stripes. Paint the door and roof line with Ultramarine.

INSIDE FRONT COVER

Note: The complete inside front and outside back covers are not pictured. The painting designs are shown on pages 22–23 and the elements appear on the step-by-step workboards on pages 20–21.

STEP ONE

Bears: Both of these bears are painted as furry bears, using Raw Sienna as a base, Brown Earth shading and Yellow Oxide and Warm White highlights.

STEP TWO

Bathers: Base paint with Aqua Green Light, then shade with a float of Teal Green. Highlight with the base colour mixed with a touch of Warm White. Paint the stripes with Ultramarine. Paint the dots with Turners Yellow using the stylus.

STEP THREE

Cap: Base the centre section, band and peak of the cap with Powder Blue. Paint the two outside sections with Turners Yellow. Shade with Ultramarine on the blue sections and Burnt Sienna on the yellow sections.

Highlight with Powder Blue and Warm White on the blue sections and Turners Yellow and Warm White on the yellow sections. Paint the button on the top with Brilliant Green.

STEP FOUR

Bucket and spade: Base paint with Country Red and shade with Burgundy. Float a little highlight with Country Red and Yellow Oxide. Paint the spade with Ultramarine and, while the paint is still wet, add a touch of Paynes Gray to shade and Powder Blue to highlight. Paint the sand with Turners Yellow and slap a touch of Warm White into this, while the paint is wet.

STEP FIVE

Lighthouse: Base paint with Warm White. With a side-load of Raw Sienna, float the shading down both sides and along the bottom edge. With the brush loaded in the same way, float in the stripes. Paint the windows with Turners Yellow outlined with Burnt Sienna. Paint the door, flag and trim around the verandah with Ultramarine. Paint the flag pole with Brown Earth.

BACK COVER

STEP ONE

Bear: Paint this bear as a Furry Bear. Base paint with Raw Sienna, and shade with Brown Earth. Highlight with Yellow Oxide and Warm White.

STEP TWO

Beach ball: Base paint with alternating stripes of Powder Blue and Turners Yellow. Float Ultramarine on the blue stripes and Turners Yellow and Warm White on the yellow stripes. Add Ultramarine dots using a stylus on the blue stripes and 'The End' with the same colour.

STEP THREE

Sunglasses: Paint the frames with Ultramarine, then pick up a touch of Powder Blue and add a little here and there. The glass is watery Burnt Umber.

SPINE OF THE BOOK

STEP ONE

The writing is Raw Sienna. Add Brown Earth liner work to the left side of each letter, then add Rich Gold lines on the right side of each letter.

STEP TWO

Paint a fine line 2.5 cm (1 in) down from the top of the spine and two fine lines 2.5 cm (1 in) in from the bottom of the spine. Make sure that these lines follow around onto the front and back of the book box. Add the year at the lower edge of the spine with Rich Gold.

FINISHING

Varnish the box inside and out.

Highlights help to separate the legs

Paint a sad facial expression on this little fellow

BEARLY BEACH
Painting Design
Note the painting design is given at half size.
Enlarge it on a photocopier at 200%.

Bearly Beach Front Cover

Bearly Beach Back Cover

BEARLY BEACH
Painting Design
Note the painting design is given at half size.
Enlarge it on a photocopier at 200%.

Bearly Beach Inside Cover

Bearly Beach Spine

MILDRED AND AMELIA

These refined young ladies have been playing dress-ups in the old lace box.
Their soft fur is very time-consuming to paint and requires many layers
of transparent paint to gradually build up the fur.

MATERIALS

Pine frame, 66 cm x 66 cm
  (26 in x 26 in)
Feathering filbert brush, ¹/₂"
Flat brushes: ¹/₄", ³/₈", ¹/₂", ⁵/₈", 1"
Short liner brush, size 1
Mop brush
Stylus
Graphite paper, White
Tracing paper
Jo Sonja's Clear Glazing Medium
Jo Sonja's Retarder
DecoArt Americana Brush 'n' Blend
Liquitex Acrylic Wood Stain:
  Dark Walnut, Cherry

Soft rags
Sandpaper, 320 grade
Jo Sonja's Artists Acrylic Gouache:
  Burnt Sienna, Brown Earth, Burnt
  Umber, Raw Sienna, Fawn, Smoked
  Pearl, Yellow Oxide, Warm White,
  Carbon Black, Teal Green,
  Pine Green
DecoArt Americana Acrylic Paint:
  Buttermilk, Sea Aqua, Dusty Rose,
  Violet Haze, Pansy Lavender,
  Antique Gold
Matisse Professional Artists Acrylic
  Colour, Burgundy
Matisse background paint, Pale Beige
Cabots Crystal Clear Satin Varnish

PREPARATION

See the painting design on page 29.

STEP ONE

Base paint the inside panel and the mat
board with two coats of Pale Beige;
sand lightly between coats.

STEP TWO

Have a small puddle of Violet Haze,
Pansy Lavender, Sea Aqua and Teal
Green on your palette and a small
container of retarder at hand.

Begin by loading the 1" flat brush
with retarder and a small amount of
Violet Haze. Gently crosshatch this
onto the background in two or three
areas, wipe the brush and do the same
with Sea Aqua, Pansy Lavender, then a
small amount of Teal Green. Softly
blend all these colours together with
the mop brush. Allow to dry.

STEP THREE

Trace the design onto tracing paper
and transfer it onto the centre board
using the graphite paper. There is no
need to transfer the dresses or flowers
at this stage.

STEP FOUR

Float a soft mixture of Violet Haze and
a touch of Teal Green onto the inside of
the mat board.

STEP FIVE

Stain the frame with a 1:1 mix of
Liquitex Dark Walnut and Cherry
stains, wiping the stain onto the frame
using the 1" flat brush. Wipe off gently
with a soft rag.

Delicate roses and lace are features of this lovely pair

BEARS

Note: The base, shade and highlight colours need to be mixed before you start to paint the bears.

COLOUR MIXES

Amelia (light bear):
- base: Raw Sienna and Fawn 2:1
- first shade: Burnt Sienna
- second shade: Burnt Sienna and Burnt Umber 1:touch
- highlight: Yellow Oxide, Fawn and Smoked Pearl 1:touch:1
- glaze: Yellow Oxide and Fawn 1:touch
- first highlight: Smoked Pearl
- second highlight: Smoked Pearl and Warm White 1:1

Mildred (dark bear):
- base: Burnt Sienna
- shade: Brown Earth and Burnt Umber 1: touch.
- highlights: Burnt Sienna and Raw Sienna 1:1
  Raw Sienna
  Raw Sienna and Fawn 1: touch
  Raw Sienna, Fawn and Smoked Pearl 1: touch:1

STEP ONE

Base paint Amelia, then float in the first shade colour. Pick up a little of the second shade colour and float a touch of this to reinforce the shadows inside the ears, at the sides of the muzzle, under the chin and on the paws and feet.

STEP TWO

Using the filbert brush very lightly, paint in the fur. Each time you pick up paint, pick up some Brush 'n' Blend as well to thin the paint. Using the first shade colour, feather in the dark fur over the shadowed areas with very light strokes which just flick the paint off. Pick up the second shade colour and repeat to reinforce the shadows.

STEP THREE

Begin to highlight the bear using the first highlight colour, flick this fur all over the bear, even on the darkest areas. These are fine, transparent lines; the gradual build-up of layers creates the effect on the finished bear.

STEP FOUR

Mix a small amount of the glaze colour with the glazing medium and wash this over the entire bear – you should still see the fur beneath this layer of glaze.

STEP FIVE

Pick up the second highlight colour and continue to flick in the fur. The highlighted areas become smaller with each change in highlight colour.

STEP SIX

Pick up the final light colour and flick this colour onto the edges of the paws, legs, feet, ears, head and muzzle.

STEP SEVEN

Using the $^5/_8$" flat brush, float a touch of Burnt Sienna around the muzzle, inside the ears and on the bottom of the feet.

MILDRED

Paint Mildred in the same way as Amelia, following the colour mixes listed for the dark bear.

EYES AND NOSES

Base paint the eyes and noses of both bears with Burnt Umber, using the liner brush. Using the $^1/_4$" flat brush, float a soft Warm White line around the left side of the eyes and a small highlight on the right side of the eyes and nose.

LACE DRESSES

STEP ONE

Trace the pattern for the dresses and bows, then transfer it onto the bears using the graphite paper.

STEP TWO

Using the liner brush and slightly watery Buttermilk, paint in all the main lace designs. With very fine crosshatched lines in Buttermilk, fill in the background and add the dots where necessary.

STEP THREE

Float Buttermilk around all the edges, washing this colour all over.

STEP FIVE

Mildred's dress: Float a touch of Violet Haze onto the flowers, Dusty Rose in the flower centres and Antique Gold onto the leaves.

STEP SIX

Amelia's dress: Float Dusty Rose onto the scrolls and Antique Gold onto the edge of the dress and sleeves.

ROSES

Paint the roses following the instructions for roses on page 14. The base colours are Buttermilk and Violet Haze, with more Violet Haze with a touch of Teal Green for the shading. Highlight the petals with Warm White. Paint the leaves with a pale mix of Pine Green, Teal Green and Buttermilk.

PANSY

Paint the pansy in Amelia's hair following the instructions on page 14. Mix Yellow Oxide, Dusty Rose and Buttermilk for the base colour. Add a touch of Burgundy to this mix for the darker shade on each petal. Highlight the tip of the petals using Buttermilk. Paint the pansy leaves with the same mix as the rose leaves.

FINISHING

STEP ONE

Using the glazing medium and a touch of Violet Haze, glaze here and there on the stained frame, then repeat using Teal Green. This should be subtle with just a hint of colour.

STEP TWO

Varnish with two or three coats.

Annette
Stevenson 1998

MILDRED AND AMELIA
Painting Design
Note the painting design is given at half size.
Enlarge it on a photocopier at 200%.

CHARLOTTE

Charlotte has beautiful soft eyes and long wispy fur. The real Charlotte, dressed just like this, sits on my bed with her portrait hanging on the wall behind her. Charlotte is an adorable bear, really soft and cute. I hope you enjoy painting her.

MATERIALS

Oval frame, 42 cm x 53 cm
   (16¹/₂ in x 21 in)
Flat brushes: ¹/₈", ¹/₄", ³/₈", ¹/₂", 1"
Rake brushes, ¹/₂" (two)
Short liner brush, size 1
J.W.'s Right Step Satin Varnish
Jo Sonja's Clear Glazing Medium
Sandpaper, 320 grade
Graphite paper, blue and white
Tracing paper
Stylus
Treasure Gold, Classic
Antiquing patina
Oil paint, Burnt Umber
Soft rags
Jo Sonja's Artists Acrylic Gouache:
   Raw Sienna, Burnt Sienna, Brown
   Earth, Gold Oxide, Yellow Oxide,
   Warm White, Burnt Umber, Pine
   Green, Teal Green, Smoked Pearl,
   Carbon Black
DecoArt Americana Acrylic Paint:
   Dusty Rose, Buttermilk
Matisse Professional Artists Acrylic
   Colour, Burgundy
Background paint, Pale Beige

PREPARATION

See the painting design on page 34.

STEP ONE

Base paint the oval insert board with two coats of Pale Beige. Sand lightly.

STEP TWO

Base paint the frame with three coats of Pale Beige. Sand well, paying part–icular attention to the routered edges.

STEP THREE

Base paint the outside edge and the small oval routered edge with two coats of Burgundy.

STEP FOUR

Trace the design, then transfer it onto the oval board, using the graphite paper. At this stage you only need to trace around the outside of the bear, her hat and the chiffon shawl.

STEP FIVE

Using watery Pale Beige and the 1" flat brush, recoat the oval board outside the design area. While this is still wet, pick up some Burgundy on the corner of the brush and place the shadow down Charlotte's left side, blending this well into the wet base colour.

Continue to add a touch of Burgundy all the way around Charlotte's outline, blending this well into the wet base coat as you go. Note that the shadows on the left side are very strong and there is just a touch of colour on the right side.

STEP SIX

Retrace the pattern for Charlotte, then transfer it onto the oval board. Trace the hat, bear, muzzle, ear and paws.

CHARLOTTE

STEP ONE

Base paint the bear in sections with Raw Sienna and glazing medium.

STEP TWO

Paint the bear following the instructions for the Shaggy Long-haired Bear on page 12, omitting the eyes at this stage. Use one of the rake brushes with a small amount of paint loaded on the tip and pulled straight to create lines of fur. Allow this to dry really well.

STEP THREE

Paint the entire bear with a coat of glazing medium. Using the second rake brush and Warm White, begin to wisp the soft fur onto the bear. Make sure that you use the brush lightly and pull the fur in the right direction. The direction of the fur around the muzzle and ears must be pulled around and down.

STEP FOUR

Base paint the eyes and nose with Brown Earth.

STEP FIVE

Recoat the bear with glazing medium. Pick up a touch of Burnt Sienna and deepen the shadows under her hat, inside her ear, under her muzzle and to separate her arm from her tummy. Pick up a small amount of Yellow Oxide and wash this colour onto her head, muzzle and body. Dry well.

STEP SIX

Apply another coat of glazing medium and continue to wisp in the extra fur using Warm White. The important thing with this step is that very small amounts of paint are applied many times to create soft, fine fur. I usually repeat this step two or three times to achieve just the right look.

STEP SEVEN

Using the ³/₈" flat brush, side-load with Burnt Umber and float down the left side of the eyes and nose. Float Raw Sienna down the right side, then touch a tiny float of Burnt Umber to the outside edges of each eye to soften.

STEP EIGHT

To finish, float a fine Warm White line onto the left side of the eye and a soft highlight onto the top right of the eye.

CHIFFON SHAWL

STEP ONE

Trace the chiffon shawl and the roses on the shawl and the hat, then transfer them using the white graphite paper.

STEP TWO

Paint the roses following the Rose instructions on page 14. The roses on Charlotte's shawl are painted using Dusty Rose and Buttermilk with a touch of Burgundy for the shade. These roses do not need final highlights.

STEP THREE

Paint the leaves using a watery mix of Pine Green and Teal Green. Where there are large gaps on the shawl, near the knot, crosshatch a touch of the rose and leaf colours.

STEP FOUR

Using the ¹/₂" flat brush and Carbon Black, softly float along all the edges of the shawl, cut in around the roses and leaves with a little of this colour and float in the fold lines.

HAT

STEP ONE

Base paint the hat with one coat of Carbon Black. Float Raw Sienna along the lower edge to form the fold in the hat.

STEP TWO

Paint the roses using Dusty Rose and Buttermilk, with Burgundy for the

shading, and Buttermilk and Warm White for the highlights. The leaves are painted using a mix of Teal Green and Buttermilk.

LACE SHAWL

STEP ONE

Trace the pattern for the lace shawl, then transfer it using the graphite paper.

STEP TWO

Using the liner brush and watery Buttermilk, paint in the lace pattern which is made up with leaves, commas, C-strokes and dots. Allow to dry.

STEP THREE

Wash Buttermilk very lightly over the entire shawl and float it around the edges.

PEARLS

STEP ONE

Trace on the line for the pearls.

STEP TWO

Base paint the pearls using the ¹/₈" flat brush with Smoked Pearl.

STEP THREE

With a brush mix of Pine Green and Smoked Pearl, float along the left edge of each pearl, then float a small amount of Warm White onto the right side of each pearl.

STEP FOUR

Float Burnt Umber on the outside, underneath each pearl. Make sure the pearls twist at the bottom.

STEP FIVE

Using the stylus, add a Warm White dot between each pearl.

FINISHING

STEP ONE

Antique the frame lightly using the antiquing patina and Burnt Umber oil paint.

STEP TWO

Rub Treasure Gold onto the routered edge of the frame, then varnish.

Try to make the roses soft and transparent

Annette
Stevenson 1998

CHARLOTTE
Painting Design
Note the painting design is given at half size.
Enlarge it on a photocopier at 200%.

RANDOLPH

I painted Randolph as a companion for Charlotte – they look just right facing each other on the wall. As yet, I have not found a bear dressed like him to sit on my bed – but I keep looking.

MATERIALS

Oval frame, 42 cm x 53 cm
 (16¹/₂ in x 21 in)
Flat brushes: ¹/₈", ¹/₄", ³/₈", ¹/₂", 1"
Short liner brush, size 1
Feathering filbert brush, ¹/₂"
Sandpaper, 320 grade
Graphite paper, blue and white
Stylus
Tracing paper
J.W.'s Right Step Satin Varnish
Antiquing patina
Oil paint, Burnt Umber
Soft rags
Treasure Gold, Classic
Jo Sonja's Artists Acrylic Gouache:
 Raw Sienna. Burnt Sienna, Brown Earth, Burnt Umber, Yellow Oxide, Fawn, Warm White, Carbon Black, French Blue, Pine Green
DecoArt Americana Acrylic Paint:
 Dusty Rose, Blue Chiffon, Light French Blue, Buttermilk
Matisse Professional Artists Acrylic
 Colour, Burgundy
Background paint, Pale Beige

PREPARATION

See the painting design on page 39.

STEP ONE

Base paint the oval insert with two coats of Pale Beige. Sand lightly.

STEP TWO

Base paint the outside of the frame with three coats of Pale Beige. Sand really well, paying particular attention to the routered edges. Base paint the outside and inside routered edges with two coats of Burgundy.

STEP THREE

Trace the design, then transfer it onto the board, using the graphite paper. At this stage, transfer only the outside edge of the hat and jacket sleeves.

STEP FOUR

Using watery Pale Beige and the 1" flat brush, recoat the oval board, outside the design area. While this is still wet, pick up some Burgundy on the corner of the brush and place the shadows around the edge of Randolph, making them deeper on his right side. The shadows need to be blended well onto the wet Pale Beige. Keep repeating this step until you are satisfied with the results.

STEP FIVE

Trace the full pattern, then transfer it onto the board. You can leave out the roses on his vest until it is base painted.

RANDOLPH

STEP ONE

Using the ¹/₂" flat brush, base paint Randolph with one coat of a 1:1 mix of Raw Sienna and Burnt Sienna.

STEP TWO

Using the same brush, float in the shadows with a 1:1 mix of Burnt Sienna

The gradual build-up of fine lines makes Randolph's fur look really soft

and Brown Earth. These are placed under the hat, inside the ear, around the muzzle, on the top and outside edges of the paws and on his tummy.

STEP THREE

Begin painting the fur using the feathering filbert brush and watery Brown Earth. Flick the fur lightly all over the bear. Repeat this step using a slightly darker shade – a 1:1 mix of Brown Earth and Burnt Umber.

STEP FOUR

Highlight the bear, using the same brush, with a gradual build-up of layers of fur. Starting with watery Raw Sienna wisp the fine fur all over the bear. This fur is also lightly painted over the dark shadow areas of the bear.

STEP FIVE

The next layer of highlight fur is painted with a 1:1 mix of Raw Sienna and Yellow Oxide. Place this layer on top of the first layer of highlight fur, but in a slightly smaller area.

STEP SIX

The final highlights are placed in an even smaller area again – the edge of the ear, top of the muzzle and a touch on the top edge of the paws. The final highlight is a watery mix of Raw Sienna, Yellow Oxide, Fawn and Warm White (1:1:touch:touch). Allow this to dry, then reassess your bear; if you feel he is too dark, add a touch more highlight.

STEP SEVEN

Eyes and nose: Paint Randolph's eyes and nose with Brown Earth. Add a small float of Raw Sienna to the right side of the eyes and nose, and a small float of Warm White to the left side of the eyes. Add a final Warm White highlight to the top right edge of the eyes and nose.

SHIRT

Using the ³⁄₈" flat brush, base paint the shirt and collar with two coats of Buttermilk. Float Raw Sienna under the chin and collar, then float a strong Warm White highlight on the collar edges.

TIE

Base paint the tie with a 2:1 mix of Burgundy and Dusty Rose. Float in the shading with a brush mix of Burgundy and Burnt Umber. Highlight the top edge of the knot with a brush mix of Dusty Rose and Burgundy. Paint the fine lines on the tie with watery Light French Blue.

VEST

STEP ONE

Base paint the vest with a 1:1 mix of Light French Blue and Blue Chiffon.

STEP TWO

Transfer the pattern for the roses and leaves onto the vest.

STEP THREE

Paint the roses following the instructions on page 14. I used a double load of Buttermilk and Dusty Rose for the base; the shading is a brush mix of Burgundy and Dusty Rose and the highlight is Buttermilk. Paint the leaves with a mix of Pine Green and Buttermilk.

STEP FOUR

Using French Blue and the ¹⁄₂" flat brush, float along the edges of the vest. With watery Light French Blue and the liner brush, paint fine lines vertically over the roses on the vest. These are painted in patches. Float a highlight of Blue Chiffon along the top edge of the vest and down the front opening.

STEP FIVE

Paint the buttons with a brush mix of Burgundy and Dusty Rose, then float a touch of Burgundy on the lower edge of each button and Dusty Rose on the top edge.

JACKET

STEP ONE

Base paint the jacket with a mix of Blue Chiffon and Light French Blue.

STEP TWO

Float the shading with Light French Blue; this needs to be really rough where the sleeves bend at the elbows.

STEP THREE

Float the highlights along the edges with Blue Chiffon, making sure that this is very well defined along the edge of the lapels and on the pocket.

STEP FOUR

Paint the 'R' on the pocket with Light French Blue, using the liner brush and painting lots of fine, horizontal lines.

HAT

Base paint the hat in Carbon Black. The hat band is base painted, shaded and highlighted using the same colours as the jacket.

FINISHING

STEP ONE

Antique the outside part of the frame, using the antiquing patina and Burnt Umber oil paint.

STEP TWO

Rub Treasure Gold onto the routered edges of the frame

STEP THREE

Varnish with two coats of of the satin varnish.

Annette
Stevenson 1999

RANDOLPH
Painting Design
Note the painting design is given at half size.
Enlarge it on a photocopier at 200%.

RAINY DAY UMBRELLA STAND

When this umbrella stand was created for me, I knew that bears playing in the rain would be the perfect painting to feature on it.

MATERIALS

Pine umbrella stand, 17 cm x 17 cm x 52 cm (6$\frac{1}{2}$ in x 6$\frac{1}{2}$ in x 20$\frac{1}{2}$ in)
Deerfoot brushes, $\frac{3}{8}$" (three)
Flat brushes: $\frac{1}{8}$", $\frac{1}{4}$", $\frac{3}{8}$", $\frac{1}{2}$"
Short liner brush, size 1
Foam brush, 2"
Jo Sonja's All-purpose Sealer
Jo Sonja's Retarder
Liquitex Acrylic Wood Stain:
    Dark Walnut, Cherry
Cotton buds
Stylus

Sandpaper, 320 grade
Tack cloth
Tracing paper
Graphite paper, white
Soft rags
Cabots Crystal Clear Satin Varnish
Varnishing brush, 1"
Jo Sonja's Artists Acrylic Gouache:
    Raw Sienna, Burnt Sienna, Brown
    Earth, Yellow Oxide, Warm White,
    Burnt Umber, Turners Yellow,
    Paynes Gray
Matisse Professional Artists Acrylic
    Colour, Burgundy
DecoArt Americana Acrylic Paint:
    Uniform Blue, Country Red

PREPARATION

See the painting designs on pages 46–48. Note that only three sides are painted.

STEP ONE

Following the instructions for the light stain on page 7, stain the umbrella stand using the foam brush. Using a soft rag, wipe lightly over the piece, following the grain of the pine. Allow this to dry, then sand lightly. Wipe well using the tack cloth or a damp rag.

STEP TWO

Using a 1:1 mix of the two stains, stain the outside again, using the foam brush.

STEP THREE

Trace the designs, then transfer them onto the sides of the umbrella stand, using the graphite paper.

PAINTING

BEARS

STEP ONE

Paint the bears, following the instructions for the Furry Bear on page 8, using Raw Sienna as the base colour, Brown Earth for shading, and Yellow Oxide and Warm White for highlights.

STEP TWO

Paint the extra liner fur, using a watery 1:3 mix of Raw Sienna and Warm White, using the liner brush.

The fine liner fur makes this little fellow look all 'roughed up'

Try to make the raindrops stand out with a float of Warm White

GUMBOOT BEAR

STEP ONE

Using the ³/₈" flat brush, base paint the raincoat with Uniform Blue and the gumboots with Turners Yellow. Base paint the umbrella with Turners Yellow and Country Red, alternating the colours.

STEP TWO

Float the shading onto the raincoat with Paynes Gray using the same brush.

STEP THREE

Using a brush mix of Uniform Blue and Warm White, float the highlights along the front edge of the coat, along the side seam, on the inside edge of the pocket and along the top and front edge of the sleeve.

STEP FOUR

Using the ¹/₈" flat brush, base paint the tabs on the front of the coat and the heart on the pocket. Float a touch of Burgundy onto the lower edge of the tabs.

STEP FIVE

Umbrella: Float Burnt Sienna shading onto the yellow sections of the umbrella. Float a highlight of Turners Yellow and Warm White onto the lower edge of the umbrella. Float Burgundy onto the Country Red sections of the umbrella, then float a highlight onto the lower edge with a brush mix of Turners Yellow and Country Red. Paint the stitching lines on the yellow sections of the umbrella with Country Red.

STEP SIX

Gumboots: Float Burnt Sienna shading onto the gumboots. Float a highlight of Turners Yellow and Warm White onto the top of the boots and around the toe of the boots. Paint the laces on the gumboots with watery Country Red with a touch of Burgundy.

STEP THREE

Base paint all the eyes and noses using Burnt Umber. Using the ¹/₈" flat brush side-loaded with Warm White, float a soft line around the left side of each eye and a touch of highlight to the top right side of the eyes and nose.

STRIPED SOU'WESTER AND YELLOW RAINCOAT

STEP ONE

Using the ¹/₂" flat brush, base paint the raincoat and the yellow sections of the hat with three coats of Turners Yellow. Base paint the brim and the blue section of the hat with Uniform Blue.

STEP TWO

With the same brush side-loaded with Burnt Sienna, float the shading onto the coat and hat, particularly under his chin, under the collar, around the outside edges of the pockets, down the front, and to section the arms from the coat.

STEP THREE

Highlight on the opposite edges using a brush mix of Turners Yellow and Warm White.

STEP FOUR

Using the ³/₈" flat brush, float the shading onto the hat using Paynes Gray. Highlight the opposite edge of the brim using a brush mix of Uniform Blue and Warm White.

STEP FIVE

Using the ¹/₈" flat brush, paint in the tabs on the front of the coat and the button on the top of the hat with Country Red.

STEP SIX

With the same brush, float a small amount of Burgundy onto the lower edge of the coat tabs and button. Paint the stitching lines on the hat and coat with watery Uniform Blue, using the liner brush.

STEP SEVEN

Umbrella handle: Base paint with Raw Sienna, using the ¼" flat brush. Float the shading down the inside edge using Brown Earth and the same brush. Highlight the outside edge, using a brush mix of Raw Sienna and Warm White.

STEP EIGHT

Umbrella knobs: Base paint with Uniform Blue, then shade with Paynes Gray. Highlight with a brush mix of Uniform Blue and Warm White. Use the ⅛" flat brush for all the shading and highlighting.

UMBRELLA BEAR

STEP ONE

Base paint the umbrella with three coats of Turners Yellow.

STEP TWO

Using the ⅜" flat brush, shade along the side with a float of Burnt Sienna, then highlight with a float of Turners Yellow and Warm White on the lower edges.

STEP THREE

Paint the knob on the top with Country Red with a small float of Burgundy on the lower edge.

STEP FOUR

Touch the tip of a cotton bud into Country Red – touch firmly onto the palette – then touch down onto the umbrella to create the dots.

Repeat, using another cotton bud and Uniform Blue, on the other sections of the umbrella.

STEP FIVE

Scarf: Base paint the scarf using the ¼" flat brush and Country Red. Shade under the chin, around the knot and down the right side of each tie with Burgundy. Highlight along the left side of the ties and the top of the knot with a mix of Country Red and Turners Yellow. Paint alternating stripes with Uniform Blue and Warm White.

PUDDLES

Mix a watery Paynes Gray, then streak this under each bear, using the ½" flat brush, while the paint is still wet. Touch a little Warm White here and there.

RAINDROPS

Using the ¼" flat brush, float around each drop with Paynes Gray. With the same brush, but using Warm White, float along the edge of each drop. Start at the top, slide down around the lower edge and slide back up to the top. Add extra Warm White highlights just inside the lower edge of each raindrop.

Using the ½" flat brush, slide on the chisel edge of the brush to form sharp straight lines diagonally across each side of the umbrella stand.

FINISHING

Varnish the umbrella stand with three coats of varnish.

Make the facial expression look a bit bedraggled

RAINY DAY UMBRELLA STAND
Painting Design
Note the painting design is given at half size.
Enlarge it on a photocopier at 200%.

RAINY DAY UMBRELLA STAND
Painting Design
Note the painting design is given at half size.
Enlarge it on a photocopier at 200%.

RAINY DAY UMBRELLA STAND
Painting Design
Note the painting design is given at half size.
Enlarge it on a photocopier at 200%.

RAINY DAY UMBRELLA

The inspiration for this umbrella came from one of my 'Thursday Girls'
(as I call them), Fay Morrison, who wanted to paint an umbrella in class.
Paint your own brolly and next time it's raining, take your bears out for a walk.

MATERIALS

Large umbrella
Jo Sonja's Textile Medium
Chalk
Deerfoot brushes, ³/₈" (three)
Flat brushes: ¹/₄", ¹/₂"
Short liner brush, size 1
Jo Sonja's Artists Acrylic Gouache:
  Raw Sienna, Brown Earth, Yellow
  Oxide, Warm White, Burnt Umber,
  Teal Green
Matisse Professional Artists Acrylic
  Colour, Burgundy
DecoArt Americana Acrylic Paint:
  Buttermilk, Mauve
Cardboard, the correct size to fit
  under a segment of the umbrella

PREPARATION

See the painting design on this page.

STEP ONE

Using chalk, draw a bear's head onto
each segment of the umbrella.

STEP TWO

On your palette, mix up a puddle of
each paint colour with an equal amount
of textile medium.

PAINTING

STEP ONE

Bears: Paint the bears in the same way
as the Furry Bear on page 8, omitting
the fine liner fur on the top.
Note: It is easier to paint the same step
on each bear all the way around, as
this gives the paint time to dry.

STEP TWO

Lace bow: Float a touch of Buttermilk
around the edges of the bow, and
crosshatch the fine lines using the
same colour. Add the scalloped edge
and dots with Buttermilk. Use the stylus
to paint the dots.

STEP THREE

Roses: Paint the roses in the same way
as the roses on page 14, with a mix
of Mauve and Buttermilk as the base
colour, side-loaded with Burgundy
for the shading and Warm White for
the highlights.
  Paint the leaves and fine squiggly
tendrils with a mix of Teal Green and
Buttermilk to finish off the rose.

FINISHING

Allow the umbrella to dry well – usually
twenty-four hours will do, then heat-set
the bears, following the instructions
on the bottle of textile medium.

RAINY DAY UMBRELLA
Painting Design
Note the painting design is given at half size.
Enlarge it on a photocopier at 200%.

Arnette
Stevenson
1998

MEDICINE CUPBOARD

These teddies are really in need of some love and a great big hug to mend all their cuts and bruises, especially the poor little fellow asleep in his mum's arms.

Sit this lovely cupboard in your bathroom and fill it with all the supplies necessary to take care of life's little accidents.

A hug and a kiss works well too.

MATERIALS

Large pine cupboard, 51 cm x 43 cm x 16 cm (20 in x 17 in x 6¼ in)
Deerfoot brushes: ³/₈" (two), ¹/₄" (three)
Flat brushes: ¹/₈", ³/₈", ¹/₂", ⁵/₈", 1"
Short liner brush, size 1
Liquitex Acrylic Wood Stain:
   Dark Walnut, Cherry
Sponge brush, 1"
Jo Sonja's Decor Crackle Medium
Stylus
Tracing paper
Graphite paper, blue
Sandpaper, 320 grade
Cabots Crystal Clear Satin Varnish
Jo Sonja's Artists Acrylic Gouache:
   Raw Sienna, Brown Earth, Fawn, Yellow Oxide, Warm White, Burnt Sienna, Burnt Umber, Smoked Pearl, Carbon Black
Matisse Professional Artists Acrylic Colour: Burgundy, Unbleached Titanium
DecoArt Americana Acrylic Paint:
   Jade Green, Buttermilk, Midnite Green

PREPARATION

See the painting design on page 56.

STEP ONE

Mix the two stain colours together in equal proportions. Stain the entire cupboard, painting the stain on using the sponge brush and brushing in the direction of the grain.

STEP TWO

Apply a thin coat of crackle medium to the centre of the door panel. This does not need to be all over – a random crackle is nice.

STEP THREE

When the crackle is just tacky, paint a thick coat of Unbleached Titanium over the centre panel.

STEP FOUR

Trace the design, then transfer it onto the centre panel of the door, using the graphite paper.

PAINTING

BEARS

These poor, sick teddies are painted in the style of the Furry Bear on page 8. Note that two of the bears have a rounded muzzle with the shading right around the edge of the muzzle.

I have used a ³/₈" deerfoot brush for the base, a ¹/₄" deerfoot brush for the shading and a ³/₈" deerfoot brush for the highlighting for the larger bears in this design.

Note: The bears are numbered 1 to 4, starting from the left.

BEAR 1

STEP ONE

Base paint, using Raw Sienna, then shade with Brown Earth. Highlight using a brush mix of Yellow Oxide and Warm White.

STEP TWO

This bear has very fine Raw Sienna and Warm White liner fur over the top of the stippled fur. Float Brown Earth on the inside of the foot pad and add a couple of brown stitching lines.

BEAR 2

Paint this bear using the smaller deerfoot brushes. Base paint using Burnt Sienna, then shade with a brush mix of Brown Earth and Burnt Umber. Highlight with the base colour and a touch of Yellow Oxide and Warm White.

BEAR 3

This cutie has a real headache. Base paint her with Yellow Oxide, then shade with Burnt Sienna. Highlight with a brush mix of Yellow Oxide and Warm White. Add some extra Warm White to the top of the ears, around the muzzle and along the edges of the arms and paws.

BEAR 4

This little baby is really feeling sick. Base paint her using Fawn, then shade with a brush mix of Fawn and Brown Earth. Highlight with a mix of Fawn and Smoked Pearl.

EYES AND NOSES

STEP ONE

All the eyes and noses are base painted using Burnt Umber. Bear 1 has oval eyes; Bear 3 has round eyes. Bears 1 and 3 have a Warm White floated line around the left side of the eyes and a small highlight on the right side of the eyes and nose.

STEP TWO

Paint Bear 2's eyes using a small flat brush. Pat the paint in rather than using conventional strokes – this way they will be an uneven shape and look like the fur is falling over them. Dry brush a Warm White highlight onto the left side of her eyes and nose.

BANDAGES

STEP ONE

Trace, then transfer all the bandages onto the bears. Base paint them all with a nice even coat of Smoked Pearl using the $^3/_8$" flat brush.

STEP TWO

Float Burnt Sienna shading onto all the bandages, then add a Warm White highlight. Be sure to curve the shading lines around the bandage on the foot and arm, so they appear to be wrapped around.

SAFETY PINS

STEP ONE

Base paint with a mix of Burnt Umber and Smoked Pearl, making a middle value grey.

STEP TWO

Using the $^1/_8$" flat brush side-loaded with Carbon Black, add a shadow here and there.

CLIP

STEP ONE

Base paint the centre elastic of the clip with Smoked Pearl and paint Warm White lines randomly over the whole area.

STEP TWO

Paint the metal clips at each end with a mix of Burnt Umber and Smoked Pearl. Add a touch of Carbon Black shading to the inside edge.

BANDAIDS

STEP ONE

Base paint with Fawn, using the $^1/_8$" flat brush.

STEP TWO

Carefully float Burnt Sienna to section off where the two Bandaids overlap. Float the same colour around the rectangle shape in the centre of the top Bandaid.

STEP THREE

Using the same brush add a small float of Smoked Pearl around the edges of both Bandaids.

BOTTLES

Epsom salts: Using the $^1/_2$" flat brush, float Midnite Green along all edges.

Paint the label with Buttermilk and the cork with Raw Sienna. Float some Brown Earth shadows onto the cork and highlight with a brush mix of Yellow Oxide and Warm White. Using the liner brush, outline the label with Burgundy and paint the writing using the same brush and colour.

Cod liver oil: Float along the edges with Burnt Umber using the $^1/_2$" flat brush. Paint the label with Buttermilk. Outline the label with Burnt Umber and paint the writing using the same colour and the liner brush. The extra liner detail on the label is painted with watery Raw Sienna.

Aspro: Float Midnite Green along all the edges. Paint the label with Jade Green and outline it with Burgundy. Paint the writing with Midnite Green, using the liner brush. Base the lid of the jar with Raw Sienna. Float the shading with Brown Earth inside the top of the lid and along the lower edge. Add a floated highlight along the edges with a brush mix of Yellow Oxide and Warm White.

WRITING

Base paint the letters using the $^3/_8$" flat brush loaded with Midnite Green. Float a brush mix of Midnite Green and Carbon Black along the left side of each letter. Float a highlight on the right side of the letters with Jade Green.

FINISHING

STEP ONE

Using the $^5/_8$" flat brush, float Burnt Umber under the bears and around the edges of the centre panel of the door.

STEP TWO

Wash Midnite Green onto the routered edges of the cupboard.

STEP THREE

Finish this medicine cupboard with three coats of varnish.

This cute little baby has really been in the wars

MEDICINE CUPBOARD
Painting Design
Note the painting design is given at half size.
Enlarge it on a photocopier at 200%.

ROSE

Rose and her baby look so forlorn; a hug would make them feel so much better.
This portrait is a sister to the one of Meg on page 61.

MATERIALS

Frame, 43 cm x 54 cm (17 in x 21¼ in)
Deerfoot brushes: ³/₈" (three),
   ¹/₄" (three)
Base-coating brush, 1"
Flat brushes: ¹/₈", ¹/₄", ¹/₂"
Short liner brush, size 1
Graphite paper, blue
Stylus
Tracing paper
Cabots Crystal Clear Satin Varnish
Sandpaper, 320 grade
Treasure Gold, Classic
Soft rags
Jo Sonja's Artists Acrylic Gouache:
   Raw Sienna, Brown Earth, Burnt
   Sienna, Yellow Oxide, Warm
   White, Fawn, Smoked Pearl, Burnt
   Umber, Teal Green, Paynes Gray
Matisse Background Paint: Pale
   Beige, Antique Green, Burgundy
DecoArt Americana Acrylic Paint:
   Buttermilk, French Mauve
Liquitex Iridescent Tinting Medium

PREPARATION

See the painting design on page 60.

STEP ONE

Base paint the frame insert with two coats of Pale Beige, sanding lightly between coats.

STEP TWO

Base paint once again with watery Pale Beige and while this is still wet, smudge Antique Green into the wet paint, using a slip-slap motion with the brush and soften where the two colours meet.

STEP THREE

Paint the frame with a watery mix of Teal Green and Paynes Gray. One coat is sufficient, as it is nice to see the grain of the pine showing through the paint. When this is dry, sand the frame back in places so that the raw wood shows through.

STEP FOUR

Trace the pattern, then transfer it onto the painting surface, using the graphite paper.

PAINTING

BEARS

Note: The bears are painted following the Furry Bear style on page 8.

STEP ONE

Rose: Base paint with Raw Sienna and Burnt Sienna brush mixed together. While this is still wet, add shade using Brown Earth and Burnt Umber; highlight using Yellow Oxide, Warm White and a touch of Burnt Sienna.

STEP TWO

Baby bear: Base paint with the smaller deerfoot brushes and Fawn. Shade with Brown Earth and highlight with a brush mix of Fawn and Smoked Pearl.

STEP THREE

Base paint the eyes and nose of each bear with Burnt Umber, using the liner brush. Using the ¹/₈" flat brush, float a small amount of Warm White onto the left side of the eyes and a tiny highlight onto the right side of the eyes and nose.

STEP FOUR

Using the highlight mix and a touch more Warm White, mix this colour with water to an ink consistency and wisp in the extra fur. Paint this fine fur in all directions, but mainly over the highlighted areas.

HAT

STEP ONE

Base paint the hat with French Mauve, then float the shading with a side-load of French Mauve and Burgundy. Have a touch of this colour where the roses are to be painted.

STEP TWO

Float the highlight using French Mauve and the Iridescent Tinting Medium.

DRESS AND HAT

STEP ONE

Base paint the dress with two smooth coats of Buttermilk. Shade with Antique Green, floating this underneath her chin, around the baby bear and around her paw. Float the pintuck lines down the front of the dress.

STEP TWO

Float a highlight with Warm White along the outside edges and to section the arms and front of her dress.

STEP THREE

Add stitching lines down each pintuck with watery Antique Green and the liner brush.

STEP FOUR

Trace the pattern for the chiffon shawl and the roses on the hat, then transfer them, using the graphite paper.

STEP FIVE

Paint the roses on the hat and shawl in the same way as the roses on page 14, using French Mauve and Buttermilk to block in the rose and French Mauve and Burgundy to shade. The first highlight is Buttermilk, then add a touch of Warm White.

STEP SIX

Paint the leaves on the shawl using Antique Green and a touch of Teal Green. Paint the leaves on the hat slightly darker.

STEP SEVEN

Float a small amount of Antique Green around the edges of the shawl, this needs to go over the roses in places but not totally cover them.

STEP EIGHT

To finish the dress, paint a very fine scalloped edge with Buttermilk along the bottom of the dress and the edge of the sleeves. Add dots with the fine end of the stylus.

STEP NINE

Add Antique Green dots along the edge of the chiffon shawl.

FINISHING

STEP ONE

Rub Treasure Gold along the outside edge of the frame.

STEP TWO

Apply two coats of varnish to the frame and the picture.

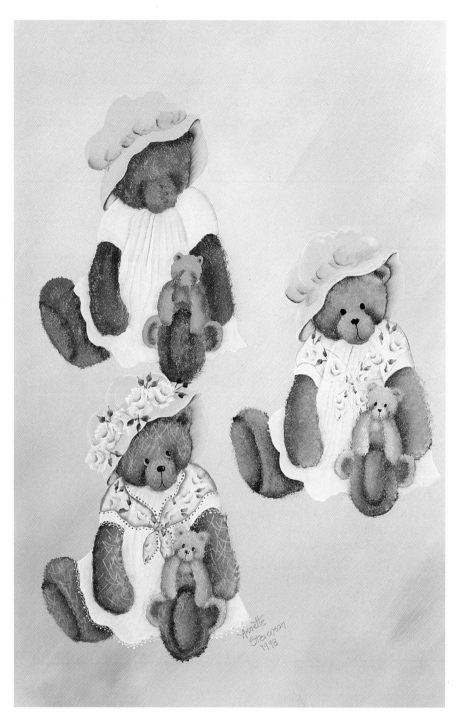

The step-by-step workboard for Rose

ROSE
Painting Design
Note the painting design is given at half size.
Enlarge it on a photocopier at 200%.

MEG

This dressed-up lady is just waiting to be given a cuddle. She has stippled fur with extra pale liner fur over the top. The shape of her muzzle makes her look very prim and proper. When framed, she and Rose on page 57 make a lovely pair.

MATERIALS

Frame, 43 cm x 54 cm (17 in x 21¼ in)
Deerfoot brushes: ³/₈" (three),
    ¹/₄" (three), ¹/₈" (one)
Flat brushes: ¹/₈", ¹/₄", ¹/₂", 1"
Short liner brush, size 1
Base-coating brush, 1"
Graphite paper, blue
Tracing paper
Cabots Crystal Clear Varnish
Matisse Background Paint, Pale Beige
Matisse Professional Artists Acrylic
    Colour: Burgundy, Antique Green
DecoArt Americana Acrylic Paint:
    Buttermilk, Dusty Rose
Jo Sonja's Artists Acrylic Gouache:
    Raw Sienna, Brown Earth, Yellow
    Oxide, Warm White, Burnt Umber,
    Fawn, Teal Green, Pine Green,
    Paynes Gray, Rich Gold, Carbon
    Black, Smoked Pearl
Sandpaper, 320 grade
Treasure Gold, Classic
Stylus
Soft rags

PREPARATION

See the painting design on page 64.

STEP ONE

Base paint the frame insert with two coats of Pale Beige, sanding lightly between coats. Base paint once again with watery Pale Beige and while this is still wet, smudge Antique Green into the wet paint, using a slip-slap motion with the brush and soften where the two colours meet.

STEP TWO

Paint the frame with a watery mix of Teal Green and Paynes Gray. One coat is sufficient, as it is nice to see the grain of the pine showing through the paint. When this is dry, sand the frame back in places so that the raw wood shows through.

STEP THREE

Trace the pattern, then transfer it onto the painting surface, using the graphite paper.

PAINTING

BEARS

Note: The bears are painted following the Furry Bear style on page 8.

STEP ONE

Base paint the bear with an equal mix of Raw Sienna and Fawn, shade with Brown Earth with a touch of Fawn and highlight with Yellow Oxide and Warm White and a touch of Fawn. Do not have the highlights too light as the wispy fur will not show up.

STEP TWO

To paint the wispy fur, add a touch more Warm White to the highlight mix and water the paint down to an ink consistency – this needs to run off the brush. Crosshatch fine lines in all directions over the top of the bear, but not too much over the shaded areas.

STEP THREE

Meg's little friend is painted in the same way as Meg, using Fawn as the base, Brown Earth as the shade, and Fawn and Smoked Pearl (brush mixed) as the highlight.

HAT

Base paint the hat with Burgundy, then float the shading using a touch of Burgundy and Burnt Umber. Highlight with a touch of Burgundy and Raw Sienna. The most important area to highlight is the brim of the hat as it comes around her head.

SHAWL

Float in the shawl with Buttermilk; float along the edges and ruffle in the lace. The little flowers that form the lace pattern are two elongated C-strokes joined together to form the flower petal. Very fine crosshatching lines fill in the background. These lines are straight not curved, as with the usual crosshatching.

CAMEO BROOCH

Base paint the cameo brooch with Smoked Pearl and float a touch of Burnt Umber around the outside edge. Using the small end of the stylus, dot Rich Gold around the outside edge. On the top of these dots, add another dot of Burnt Umber.

The tiny little bear's head is painted using the ¹/₈" deerfoot brush. Base with Raw Sienna, then shade using Brown Earth and highlight with a brush mix of Yellow Oxide and Warm White.

LITTLE BEAR'S HAT

The little bear's hat is painted using Teal Green, highlighted with a float of Teal Green and Buttermilk.

ROSES

The roses on the shawl are painted in the same way as the large roses on page 14. Use a $^1/_8$" flat brush with watery paint. Once the roses are dry, float a touch of Carbon Black around the edges of the shawl.

The roses on Meg's hat are painted using Raw Sienna and Buttermilk to block in the rose, then add a touch more Raw Sienna in the throat of the rose and around the lower edge of the bowl. Use Warm White to highlight the petals. Paint the leaves using Pine Green with a touch of Buttermilk.

PANSIES

Using Paynes Gray and Burgundy, mix a nice purple. Add a touch of Buttermilk to some of the mix so that you have two values of this colour. Using the $^1/_2$" flat brush, stroke in the petals following the step-by-step workboard (right).

EYES AND NOSES

The eyes and noses on these bears are painted with Burnt Umber. They are round. Float a very small line of Warm White along the left side of each eye and a small highlight on the right side of the eyes and nose.

FINISHING

STEP ONE

Rub Treasure Gold around the outside edge of the frame.

STEP TWO

Apply two coats of varnish to the painting and the frame.

The step-by-step workboard for Meg

MEG
Painting Design
Note the painting design is given at half size.
Enlarge it on a photocopier at 200%.

MISS MOLLY AND SIR DANIEL

This cupboard is one of my favourite pieces. It sits in our entrance hall with two of my favourite bears perched on top. It is another fantastic piece from my 'wood man' David.

MATERIALS

Pine cupboard, 48 cm x 82 cm x
    30 cm (19 in x 32 in x 12 in)
Feathering filbert brush, ¹/₂"
Flat brushes: ¹/₄", ³/₈", ⁵/₈", 1"
Deerfoot brush, ¹/₈"
Short liner brush, size 1
Foam brush, 2"
DecoArt Americana Brush 'n' Blend
DecoArt Gel Stain, Oak
Jo Sonja's Artists Acrylic Gouache:
    Raw Sienna, Burnt Sienna, Fawn,
    Burnt Umber, Yellow Oxide, Warm
White, Smoked Pearl, Brown Earth,
    Paynes Gray, Carbon Black,
    French Blue, Teal Green, Rich Gold
DecoArt Americana Acrylic Paints:
    Buttermilk, Light French Blue,
    Blue Chiffon
Matisse Professional Artists Acrylic
    Colour, Burgundy
Cabots Crystal Clear Satin Varnish
Clear glazing medium
Graphite paper, white
Tracing paper
Stylus
Sandpaper, 320 grade
Rags for staining

PREPARATION

See the painting design on the Pull Out Pattern Sheet.

STEP ONE

Stain the entire cupboard with a coat of the oak stain, brushing it on following the grain of the wood. Wipe off gently with a rag. When the stain is dry, sand the edges heavily to reveal the raw wood beneath.

STEP TWO

Using watery Light French Blue and a touch of Paynes Gray, paint the frame around the doors and the top routered edge. When dry, sand in places to reveal the raw wood.

STEP THREE

Trace the design for Miss Molly and Sir Daniel onto tracing paper, then transfer them onto the cupboard doors, using the graphite paper.

PAINTING

BEARS

Note: These two bears are painted in the same style as Mildred and Amelia on page 24, using slightly different colours. Have the following colours already mixed on your palette before you begin painting:
- base: Raw Sienna and Fawn 2:1
- first shade: Burnt Sienna
- second shade: Burnt Sienna and Burnt Umber 1:touch
- highlight: Yellow Oxide, Fawn and Smoked Pearl 1:touch:1

Gradually build layers of fur to create these soft-looking bears

- glaze: Yellow Oxide and Fawn 1:touch
- first highlight: Yellow Oxide and Smoked Pearl 1:1
- second highlight: Smoked Pearl
- third highlight: Smoked Pearl and Warm White 1:1

MISS MOLLY

STEP ONE

Base paint the dress using a mix of Blue Chiffon and Light French Blue. Float the shadows and folds for her dress with Light French Blue. I have used the ⁵/₈" flat brush but if you are more comfortable using a smaller brush, then do so.

STEP TWO

Highlight the dress with a float of Warm White.

STEP THREE

Using the ³/₈" flat brush side-loaded with Warm White, add the ruffled edge to the hem of the skirt, edges of the sleeves and around her neck.

STEP FOUR

Trace the pattern for the shawl and the cameo, then transfer them onto the bear, over her dress, using the graphite paper.

STEP FIVE

The shawl is painted with a thick coat of Light French Blue. While this paint is still wet, fully load the ³/₈" flat brush with French Blue and Paynes Gray. Paint in the crossed pattern on the shawl using the chisel edge firmly. Float a touch of Paynes Gray to shade. The fringing is painted with Light French Blue first, then a touch of Paynes Gray.

CAMEO

STEP ONE

Base paint the cameo with Smoked Pearl and add shading around the edge with Burnt Umber.

STEP TWO

Paint the little bear's head, using the deerfoot brush, wiping the colour off the brush between colours. Base paint with Raw Sienna, shade with Brown Earth and highlight with Warm White and Yellow Oxide.

STEP THREE

Using the stylus, add Burnt Umber dots around the edge. When these are dry, add Rich Gold dots on top of them. Press down really hard to break the first layer of dots.

HAT

STEP ONE

Paint the hat using Blue Chiffon, shaded with Light French Blue.

STEP TWO

With Warm White, float a scallop around the brim of the hat and add fine crosshatching lines.

STEP THREE

Outline the fine pieces of netting on the hat underneath the pansies with Warm White and crosshatch with the same colour.

SHOES

Base paint with Carbon Black, then highlight with a side-loaded float of Light French Blue. Paint the stitching lines and dots in the same colour. Paint the buckle with the liner brush using Light French Blue with a touch of Paynes Gray.

SIR DANIEL

STEP ONE

Base paint the jacket with a mix of Light French Blue and French Blue mixed together.

STEP TWO

Pick up a touch of French Blue and Paynes Gray on the side of the brush and float the shading. When floating, lift the brush occasionally to create a rough line – this enhances the edge of the clothes.

STEP THREE

Float the highlights along the edges of the jacket and on the top of the folds, using a brush mix of Light French Blue and Blue Chiffon.

TROUSERS

Base paint with a coat of French Blue, then softly shade with Paynes Gray. Highlight the edges of the trousers with a touch of Light French Blue, paying particular attention to the front seam and the front leg of the trousers.

BOOTS

STEP ONE

Paint the boots with two coats of Brown Earth and shade with Burnt Umber, making sure there is a definite line between the two boots.

STEP TWO

Highlight with a mix of Burnt Sienna and Raw Sienna, strengthened with extra Raw Sienna.

STEP THREE

Paint the laces with the liner brush double-loaded with Raw Sienna and Burnt Umber.

PANSIES

Paint the pansies following the instructions on page 14, using the same colours: mixes of Burgundy, Paynes Gray and Buttermilk. The leaves and stems are a mix of Teal Green and Buttermilk.

FINISHING

Give this cute little cupboard four coats of varnish with a light sand between coats.

Annette
Stevenson
1999

HEIRLOOM HAT BOX

This beautiful large pine hat box is absolutely covered in bears – furry ones, long-haired ones and really old ones. This piece is suitable for a confident beginner. It is a real challenge; once you start, however, I'm sure you will not put your brushes down until you are finished.

MATERIALS

Large pine hat box
Flat brushes: $^1/_4$", $^1/_2$", $^3/_8$"
Dagger brushes: $^3/_8$" (three), $^1/_4$" (three)
Short liner brush, size 1
Rake brushes, $^3/_8$" (two)
Round brush, size 2
Sponge brush, 1"
Stylus
Good quality paper towel
Liquitex Acrylic Wood Stain:
    Dark Walnut, Cherry
Jo Sonja's Clear Glazing Medium
Liquitex Iridescent Tinting Medium
Jo Sonja's Artists Acrylic Gouache:
    Raw Sienna, Brown Earth, Yellow
    Oxide, Burnt Sienna, Burnt Umber,
    Warm White, Fawn, Pine Green,
    Jade Green, Paynes Gray
Matisse Professional Artists Acrylic
    Colour, Burgundy
DecoArt Americana Acrylic Paint,
    Buttermilk
Jo Sonja's Retarder
All-purpose sealer
Cabots Crystal Clear Satin Varnish
Tracing paper
Graphite paper, white
Sandpaper, 320 grade

PREPARATION

See the painting design on the Pull Out Pattern Sheet.

STEP ONE

Stain the entire hat box following the instructions for a light stain on page 7. Using the sponge brush, apply a coat of the two Liquitex stains mixed to-gether to the outside of the box only, following the wood grain.

STEP TWO

Trace the design for the bears, then transfer it, using the graphite paper, onto the sides and lid of the box.

PAINTING

Note: This box is easier to do if all the bears are painted first and the same types of bears are painted together; for example, paint all the furry ones then the long-haired ones, then all the old worn-out bears.

The bears are numbered on the pattern sheet and are painted in the following styles:

Lid (from left to right): Bear 1 (furry), Bear 2 (furry), Bear 3 (long-haired), Bear 4 (old), Bear 5 (long-haired),
Sides (from the right of the writing): Bears 2, 3, 7, 8, 9 and 11 (furry), Bears 1, 4 and 6 (long-haired), Bears 5 and 10 (old)

BEARS

STEP ONE

Note: All the long-haired and old bears are painted in the same way as in the basic instructions for that style of bear. The colours for the furry bears differ slightly.

Bears 2, 9 and 11 on the sides: (mustard colour) base paint in Raw Sienna, shade with Brown Earth and highlight with Yellow Oxide and Warm White.

Bear 3 on the side and Bear 2 on the lid: base paint with Yellow Oxide, shade with Burnt Sienna and highlight with a mix of Yellow Oxide and Warm White.

Bear 1 on the lid and Bear 8 on the side: base paint with a mix of Burnt Sienna and Raw Sienna, shade with a mix of Brown Earth and Burnt Umber and highlight with Yellow Oxide, Burnt Sienna and Warm White.

Bear 7 on the side: base paint with Fawn, shade with Brown Earth and highlight with a mix of Fawn and Warm White.

STEP TWO

Paint all the eyes and noses with Burnt Umber and highlight them with Warm White.

LID DETAILS

STEP ONE

Bear 1: Base paint the bow with Burgundy. Side-load a size $^3/_8$" flat brush with a mix of Burgundy and Buttermilk. Float in highlights to separate the different parts of the bow. The lace edge and dots are painted with Jade Green, using the large end of the stylus to paint the dots.

STEP TWO

Bear 3: Float in the hat using Butter-milk. Mix Pine Green and a touch of Buttermilk with the tinting medium and base paint the bow and ribbons. High-light the edges of the ribbons and the top of the bow with straight Iridescent Tinting Medium. Paint the roses using Raw Sienna and Buttermilk for the base, shade with Raw Sienna and high-light with Warm White. The leaves are Pine Green and Buttermilk.

STEP THREE

Bear 5: Mix some Pine Green, Brown Earth and a touch of Buttermilk and base paint his jumper with this mix. Shade with a float of Pine Green and Brown Earth to separate the sleeves from the body and under the chin. Highlight with a mix of the base colour and a touch of Buttermilk. Trace the heart and transfer it onto his jumper or paint it freehand. Base paint the heart with Burgundy; paint the writing with Buttermilk.

STEP FOUR

Lace tablecloth: Using a $^3/_8$" dagger brush, float in all edges of the table-cloth. Float in the inner scallops as C-strokes. Using the liner brush, start the crosshatching; there is a lot to do, so take the time to study the picture and pattern carefully to make sure that the lace is correct. Finish with dots, using the stylus.

SIDE DETAILS

STEP ONE

Bear 1: Float in the lace collar and bow, add crosshatching lines and dots using Buttermilk.

STEP TWO

Bear 2: Base paint the bow with Burgundy, highlight with a mix of Burgundy and Buttermilk. Add the checked lines using the colour mixed for the jumper from the lid.

STEP THREE

Bear 3: Base the bow with the jumper mix and shade using Pine Green. Highlight with a mix of Pine Green and Buttermilk. The lines are painted with Burgundy.

STEP FOUR

Bear 4: Float the lace shawl and bow with Buttermilk, using the dagger brush. Add lines and dots, then paint a small rose in the middle of the bow and another one on her shoulder.

STEP FIVE

Bear 6: Base paint her hat with Burgundy, then shade with a mix of Burgundy and Burnt Umber. Highlight with a mix of Burgundy and Buttermilk.

STEP SIX

Bear 7: Float in her headband and bow with Buttermilk, then add crosshatching lines and dots with the same colour. Place a small rose and leaves in the middle of the bow using the $^1/_4$" flat brush.

STEP SEVEN

Bear 8: Base paint the bow with Paynes Gray, highlight with Paynes Gray and Buttermilk. Add lines using the same mix.

STEP EIGHT

Bear 9: Float in the collar with Buttermilk and paint in the crosshatching lines in the same colour. The bow tie is Burgundy with a floated highlight of Burgundy and Buttermilk. Add the dots with the stylus, using Buttermilk.

FINISHING

Finish with a couple of coats of varnish and sit this box somewhere special for everyone to admire.

Fine lines and dots create the lace on the lid

Cuddly bears on the side of the hat box

2

Annette
96

3

Annette
96

TEDDIES TEA PARTY

I have painted this design using lots of green, yellow and burgundy to match my room, but the design would look just as nice painted in colours to match your own decor.

MATERIALS

Butler's tray, 42 cm x 64 cm
(16½ in x 25 in)
Deerfoot brushes: ¼" (three),
³⁄₈" (three)
Flat brushes: ⅛", ¼", ½"
Short liner brush, size 1
Base-coating brush, 1"
Sponge brush, 1"
Sandpaper, 320 grade and sanding
block
Candle (any colour)
Masking tape
Cabots Crystal Clear Satin Varnish
Tracing paper
Graphite paper, white and blue
Tack cloth
Soft rags
Stylus
Jo Sonja's Clear Glazing Medium
Liquitex Wood Stain: Dark Walnut,
Cherry
Jo Sonja's Artists Acrylic Gouache:
Raw Sienna, Burnt Sienna, Brown
Earth, Burnt Umber, Yellow Oxide,
Warm White, Fawn, Smoked Pearl,
Pine Green, Green Oxide,
Carbon Black
Jo Sonja's Background Paint, Primrose
Matisse Professional Artists Acrylic
Colour, Burgundy
DecoArt Americana Acrylic Paint:
Buttermilk, Country Red

PREPARATION

See the painting design on the Pull Out
Pattern Sheet.

STEP ONE

Base paint the entire tray with two
coats of Pine Green, sanding lightly
between coats. Wipe with the tack cloth.

STEP TWO

Using the masking tape, mask off the
centre of the tray, leaving about 2.5 cm
(1 in) all around the base of the tray.

STEP THREE

Hold the candle firmly in your hand
and rub vigorously all over the sides
and edges of the tray. Try to rub the
candle in the same direction on each
surface of the tray.

STEP FOUR

Base paint over the waxed areas with a
thick coat of Primrose. Allow to dry.

STEP FIVE

Sand vigorously to remove the paint
from over the wax. (A sanding block
makes sanding in the corners easier.)
Remove the tape.

STEP SIX

Trace the design for the bears, clothes
and the picnic rug, then transfer it onto
the tray, using the graphite paper.

PAINTING

Note: The bears are all painted following the instructions for the Furry Bear
on page 8. Working from left to right
the bears are numbered 1 to 7.

BEAR 1

Base paint with a brush mix of Raw Sienna and Yellow Oxide, shade with
Burnt Sienna; highlight with a brush
mix of Yellow Oxide and Warm White.

BEAR 2

Base paint with Raw Sienna, then
shade with Brown Earth. Highlight with
Yellow Oxide and Warm White. This
bear has extra liner fur over the top,
painted with a watery mix of Raw
Sienna and Warm White.

BEAR 3

Base paint this bear with a brush mix of
Raw Sienna and Burnt Sienna, then
shade with an equal mix of Brown
Earth and Burnt Umber. Highlight with
a brush mix of Yellow Oxide, Burnt
Sienna and Warm White, making an
apricot colour.

BEAR 4

Base paint the bear with Fawn, shade
with a brush mix of Fawn and Brown
Earth. Highlight with Fawn and
Smoked Pearl, then with a touch more
Smoked Pearl.

BEAR 5

Base paint this chubby fellow with
Burnt Sienna, then shade with Brown
Earth and Burnt Umber. Highlight with
Yellow Oxide. With watery Yellow
Oxide, add some wispy liner fur over
the highlighted areas.

BEAR 6

I find it easier to use the smaller
deerfoot brushes for this little cutie.
Base paint the bear with Yellow Oxide.
Shade with Burnt Sienna and highlight
with a brush mix of Yellow Oxide and
Warm White.

BEAR 7

Base paint with Raw Sienna, then shade
with Brown Earth. Highlight with a mix
of Yellow Oxide and Warm White. The
wispy liner fur is painted with watery
Yellow Oxide and Warm White – a touch
lighter in value than the highlight mix.

EYES AND NOSES

Base paint all the eyes and noses with Burnt Umber using the 1/8" flat brush. Float Warm White onto the left side of each eye and add a small Warm White highlight to the right side of the eyes and noses.

CLOTHES AND ACCESSORIES

Note: All the shading and highlighting on the clothes is painted using a side-loaded flat brush and floating the colours into place.

T-SHIRT

STEP ONE

Base paint the T-shirt using the 1/2" flat brush with two coats of Buttermilk.

STEP TWO

Using the same brush, float Green Oxide under the chin and to section the sleeves from the tummy part of the T-shirt.

STEP THREE

Using the 1/4" flat brush, paint in the stripes with Green Oxide. On the corner of the brush, pick up a touch of Pine Green and float some darker

Use the smaller deerfoot brushes for this dear little bear

shading on these stripes. Float a Warm White highlight onto the Buttermilk stripes. Paint a fine Burgundy line on both edges of the green stripes and a Yellow Oxide line on both edges of the Buttermilk stripes. For fine lines, it helps to water down the paint and to stay on the tip of the brush.

TIE

STEP ONE

Base paint the tie with Burgundy. With Burnt Umber, float shading under the chin, around the knot and down the right-hand side. Using the 1/2" flat brush, float a strong highlight of Country Red onto the opposite edges.

STEP TWO

Paint the star pattern using the liner brush with Buttermilk. Paint fine lines intersecting in the middle with a Green Oxide dot in the centre.

CAP

STEP ONE

Base paint with brush-mixed Yellow Oxide and Warm White. Shade with Raw Sienna and highlight with a lighter mix of the base colour.

STEP TWO

Paint the small button on top with Green Oxide, then shade with Pine Green. Paint the stitching lines with Green Oxide.

SCARF

Paint the scarf with Buttermilk, float the shading with Green Oxide and highlight with Warm White. Paint the checks with watery Burgundy.

LACE COLLAR

STEP ONE

Using the 1/2" flat brush, pick up a small amount of Green Oxide, then a touch of Buttermilk on the corner of the brush. Blend this well on the palette, then

float around the edges of the collar and float a touch under the chin.

STEP TWO

Using the liner brush and the same colour, crosshatch the collar and add a fine scalloped edge. Paint little yellow dots along the scalloped edge with the stylus.

OVERALLS

STEP ONE

Even though the background is Pine Green, base paint again with this colour, shade with brush-mixed Pine Green and Burnt Umber. Highlight with a float of Green Oxide.

STEP TWO

Paint the small bear's head with Raw Sienna, shade with Brown Earth and Yellow Oxide, then highlight with Warm White. I have painted this bear using the liner brush, wiping the brush on the paper towel between each colour change.

STEP THREE

Paint the stitching lines with a watery mix of Green Oxide and Buttermilk. Paint the buttons with Raw Sienna and Burnt Umber dots.

DRESS

STEP ONE

Base paint the dress with Buttermilk and shade with a mix of Buttermilk and Yellow Oxide.

STEP TWO

Float the frill along the lower edge of the dress and on the sleeves with Buttermilk. Add tiny Warm White dots along the edges, using the end of the stylus.

STEP THREE

Paint the heart on the bodice and the stitching lines using the liner brush and Green Oxide.

HAT

Base paint with Green Oxide, then shade with Pine Green. Float a small highlight with Green Oxide and Buttermilk along the edge of the brim and the top of the hat.

VEST

Base paint with Burgundy, then shade with a float of Burnt Umber. Highlight with a strong float of Country Red. Paint the buttons with Green Oxide and add Buttermilk dots, using the stylus.

PICNIC RUG

STEP ONE

Using the largest flat brush that you are comfortable working with, base paint the entire rug with two coats of Buttermilk.

STEP TWO

Using the 1/2" flat brush, paint the wide stripes with a 1:1 mix of Green Oxide and glazing medium. Apply even pressure as you paint along the stripe.

STEP THREE

Paint a fine Green Oxide line on top of each large stripe and a Yellow Oxide line on the lower edge.

STEP FOUR

With a brush mix of Pine Green and Burnt Umber, float under the bears, wiggle the brush as you float to give the fur an uneven edge. Some of this colour can also be streaked across the rug.

STEP FIVE

Paint the lace edge with watery Buttermilk, painting the fine line first, then adding the crosses, then the dots.

THE PICNIC

Trace the design for the honey pot, basket of cherries, plate of choc-chip cookies, lollipop, teapot, and cup and saucer, then transfer them onto the rug using the blue graphite paper.

HONEY POT

STEP ONE

Paint with Raw Sienna, then float Brown Earth along all edges and into the inside of the pot. Float a small highlight along the top rim of the pot, using a brush mix of Raw Sienna and Buttermilk.

STEP TWO

Paint the spoon and the label with Buttermilk, add a small float of Raw Sienna along the left side of both the label and spoon. Paint a fine Burgundy line outlining the label and two fine Burgundy lines on the spoon handle. Paint the writing with Green Oxide and a fine line on either side of the Burgundy lines on the spoon, using the same colour.

BASKET OF CHERRIES

STEP ONE

Paint the basket with Raw Sienna, then float a touch of Brown Earth under each loop of the basket weave. Add a small line in Brown Earth to section the basket weave.

STEP TWO

Using the 1/4" flat brush loaded with Yellow Oxide and tipped with Warm White, dry-brush across each loop in the weave.

STEP THREE

Paint the cherries with Country Red, then shade with Burgundy. The shading is a tiny C-stroke in the top of the cherries and along the bottom edge of each cherry.

STEP FOUR

Using the 1/8" flat brush side-loaded in a mix of Yellow Oxide and Country Red, float a highlight to define the top of each cherry. Add the stalks with Burnt Umber.

CHOC-CHIP COOKIES

STEP ONE

Base paint the plate with a medium value grey – a mix of Carbon Black and Warm White. Base paint the cookies with Raw Sienna.

STEP TWO

Float Burnt Umber shading underneath the cookies and at the base of the plate.

STEP THREE

Float Warm White along the top edge of the plate. Stipple Warm White onto the centre of each cookie and paint the choc-chips with a dot of Burnt Umber. Float Brown Earth around the edge of each cookie.

TEA SET

STEP ONE

Base paint the teapot, tea cup and saucer with two coats of Buttermilk, then float the shading with a brush mix of Burnt Umber and Raw Sienna. Highlight the edges with Warm White. Paint the lines with Burgundy and the dots with Green Oxide.

LOLLIPOP

Paint the stick with Raw Sienna and the lollipop with Warm White with a Country Red swirl.

FINISHING

STEP ONE

Stain the tray legs with an equal mix of the two stains. Wipe off gently with a soft rag.

STEP TWO

Varnish the tray with four coats of varnish, then stand the tray on its legs for everyone to admire.